Purpose Poetry

Book 1

Years 1-2

Creative ideas to develop a love of language

Suzi de Gouveia

C000177455

ential
urces

essential
resources

Title: Purposeful Poetry
Creative ideas to develop a love of language
Book 1: Years 1–2

Author: Suzi de Gouveia

Editor: Marie Langley

Layout: Jackie Andrews

Book Code: 161A

ISBN: 978-1-877498-08-4

Published: 2008

Publisher: Essential Resources Educational Publishers Limited

United Kingdom Office	*Australian Office*	*New Zealand Office*
Units 8–10 Parkside	PO Box 90	PO Box 5036
Shortgate Lane	Oak Flats	Invercargill
Laughton	NSW 2529	p: 0800 087 376
BN8 6DG	p: 1800 005 068	f: 0800 937 825
p: 0845 3636 147	f: 1800 981 213	
f: 0845 3636 148		

Website: www.essentialresourcesuk.com

Copyright: Text: © Suzi de Gouveia, 2008
Edition and Illustrations:
© Essential Resources Educational Publishers Limited, 2008

The Author: Suzi de Gouveia is a full-time classroom teacher with a passion for language and creativity. She has developed this resource through a desire to foster such a passion in her pupils. This book is dedicated to her Mum, Jeanne Beauchamp, who is a word whizz and who wrote a number of the poems in this book.

Acknowledgements:

Essential Resources would like to acknowledge the following anonymous poems; *Grasshopper Green*, page 8; *Five Little Mice*, page 26; *Peep in the Basket*, page 29; *Mr Nobody*, page 11; *The Dog and the Bee*, page 14; *Open Sesame*, page 17; *A Smile*, page 20; *The Parrot*, page 23.

Photocopy Notice:
Permission is given to schools and teachers who buy this book to reproduce it (and/or any extracts) by photocopying or otherwise, but only for use at their present school. Copies may not be supplied to anyone else or made or used for any other purpose.

Contents

INTRODUCTION

This book was developed through a desire to foster a love of language in a creative and interesting way in my classroom. This use of poetry has worked beyond my wildest dreams: my pupils take great pride in their poetry books. Each week we work on a new poem. By the time Friday arrives, the children are asking, *"What will we be doing for our poetry response?"*

I have even had parents say,
"He is not too well today but he refused to stay at home because he did not want to miss out on your poetry response!"

To me, that is success!

It is simple to create this interest. Follow these steps:

1. Use the 'Oral Language Plan: Poetry' for the poem you have chosen.
2. Do the prediction activity.
3. Read the poem from an enlarged copy and display this copy for the week.
4. Give the children a copy of the poem each to stick into their poetry books.
5. Encourage the children to read the poem as part of their homework.
6. Read the poem each day and then lead the children through the suggested discussions. The processes of Critical Thinking, Exploring Language and Processing Information are covered through these discussions.
7. Encourage the children to use the words from the poem; soon this richer vocabulary will be used in other oral and written language activities.
8. The response to the poem on a Friday is the highlight of the week. These responses are designed to provide the opportunity to develop fine motor skills through colouring, cutting, tracing, painting, and so on.
9. The activity is modelled to the pupils in the class Poetry Book (a scrapbook is a good size for this one).
10. The children do their own version of the activity in their own poetry book.

Build up a stock of paints, oil pastels, chalks, paper and plastic, string, wool, wax crayons, pipe cleaners and glue to have on hand so you don't have to go rushing around to get the things you need. Keep an eye out for bargains!

I have found the easiest way to organise paint is to buy some plastic drinking cups and put an infant colour block in each one. When needed, you add a few drops of water and a paintbrush. The children paint and, when finished, all that needs to be done is to wash the brush—no need to clean up messy paint holders!

A term planning sheet has been included on pages 5 and 6. Copy the sheet to keep in your planning folder and just fill in the titles of the poems.

© Essential Resources Educational Publishers Ltd, 2008

POETRY UNIT PLAN

Curriculum areas: *Literacy; Art and design*   **YEAR 1 Term:**

LEARNING OBJECTIVES

LITERACY

5. Word recognition: decoding (reading)
- Recognise alternative ways of spelling phonemes and begin to know which words contain which spelling alternatives.
- Identify the constituent parts of two-syllable and three-syllable words to support the application of phonic knowledge and skills.
- Recognise automatically an increasing number of familiar high frequency words.
- Apply phonic knowledge and skills as the prime approach to reading unfamiliar words that are not completely decodable.
- Read more challenging texts which can be decoded using their acquired phonic knowledge and skills, along with automatic recognition of high frequency words.
- Read phonically decodable two-syllable and three-syllable words.

7. Understanding and interpreting texts
- Identify the main events and characters in stories, and find specific information in simple texts.
- Use syntax and context when reading for meaning.
- Make predictions showing an understanding of ideas, events and characters.
- Recognise the main elements that shape different texts.
- Explore the effect of patterns of language and repeated words and phrases.

8. Engaging with and responding to texts
- Visualise and comment on events, characters and ideas, making imaginative links to their own experiences.

ART AND DESIGN

Exploring and developing ideas
1. Pupils should be taught to:
   a) record from first-hand observation, experience and imagination, and explore ideas.

Investigating and making art, craft and design
2. Pupils should be taught to:
   c) represent observations, ideas and feelings, and design and make images and artefacts.

Breadth of study
5. During the key stage, pupils should be taught the knowledge, skills and understanding through:
   c) using a range of materials and processes

UNIT EVALUATION

WEEK	POEM	WEEK	POEM	WEEK	POEM
1		6		11	
2		7		12	
3		8		13	
4		9		14	
5		10		15	

© Essential Resources Educational Publishers Ltd, 2008

POETRY UNIT PLAN

Curriculum areas: *Literacy; Art and design*   **YEAR 2 Term:**

LEARNING OBJECTIVES

LITERACY

5. Word recognition: decoding (reading)
- Read independently and with increasing fluency longer and less familiar texts.
- Know how to tackle unfamiliar words that are not completely decodable.
- Read less common alternative graphemes including trigraphs.
- Read high and medium frequency words independently and automatically.

7. Understanding and interpreting texts
- Draw together ideas and information from across a whole text, using simple signposts in the text.
- Give some reasons why things happen or characters change.
- Explain organisational features of texts, including alphabetical order, layout, diagrams, captions, hyperlinks and bullet points.
- Use syntax and context to build their store of vocabulary when reading for meaning.
- Explore how particular words are used, including words and expressions with similar meanings.

8. Engaging with and responding to texts
- Engage with books through exploring and enacting interpretations.
- Explain their reactions to texts, commenting on important aspects.

ART AND DESIGN

Exploring and developing ideas
1. Pupils should be taught to:
    a) record from first-hand observation, experience and imagination, and explore ideas.

Investigating and making art, craft and design
2. Pupils should be taught to:
    c) represent observations, ideas and feelings, and design and make images and artefacts.

Breadth of study
5. During the key stage, pupils should be taught the knowledge, skills and understanding through:
    —c) using a range of materials and processes

UNIT EVALUATION

WEEK	POEM	WEEK	POEM	WEEK	POEM
1		6		11	
2		7		12	
3		8		13	
4		9		14	
5		10		15	

Oral Language Plan : Poetry

Title: *Grasshopper Green*   **Term:** _____ **Week:** _____

Monday	**Prediction:**
Critical Thinking	What kind of creature is a grasshopper? What do you know about these creatures?

Tuesday	**Terminology:**
Exploring Language	Poem, verse, anthology.
	Vocabulary Development:
	Interest words: comical, fare, meadow, hedgerow, beautiful. Contractions: summer's, it's. Compound words: hedgerow, grasshopper, grandmother. Singular/plural: spider/s, grasshopper/s, child/ren. Antonyms: bright—dull, out—in, high—low, beautiful—ugly. Homonyms: fare—fair, sun—son. Synonyms: fun—excitement, joy, happiness …

Wednesday	**Print Conventions:**
	Capital letters for proper nouns and beginning of sentences, dash, apostrophe, comma, full stop.

Thursday	**Phonological Patterns:**
	Word family: un—fun, sun, bun … Blend: gr—green, grass, grab … Suffix: ing—playing … Rhyming words: chap—cap, fare—wear, sun—fun, house—mouse. gay—way, know—low.

Friday	**Visual Information:**
Processing Information	Discuss the presentation used for "hopperty", "high", "low" and "little" to denote the movement, position and size.
	Response:
	Use the template on page 9 to copy a grasshopper for each child. Colour and cut out the body and legs. Attach legs to the body with paper fasteners. Prepare the page by drawing grass and sun, using oil pastels. Dye the sky blue. Stick the grasshopper body onto picture, leaving the legs free to move.

                                    © Essential Resources Educational Publishers Ltd, 2008

Grasshopper Green

Grasshopper Green is a comical chap;

He lives on the best of fare.

Bright little trousers, jacket and cap,

These are his summer wear.

Out in the meadow he loves to go,

Playing away in the sun;

It's hopperty, skipperty, high and low_

Summer's the time for fun.

Grass hopper Green has a quaint little house;

It's under the hedgerow gay.

Grandmother Spider, as still as a MOUSE,

Watches him over the way.

Gladly he's calling the children, I know,

Out in the beautiful sun.

It's hopperty, skipperty, high and low_

Summer's the time for fun.

© Essential Resources Educational Publishers Ltd, 2008

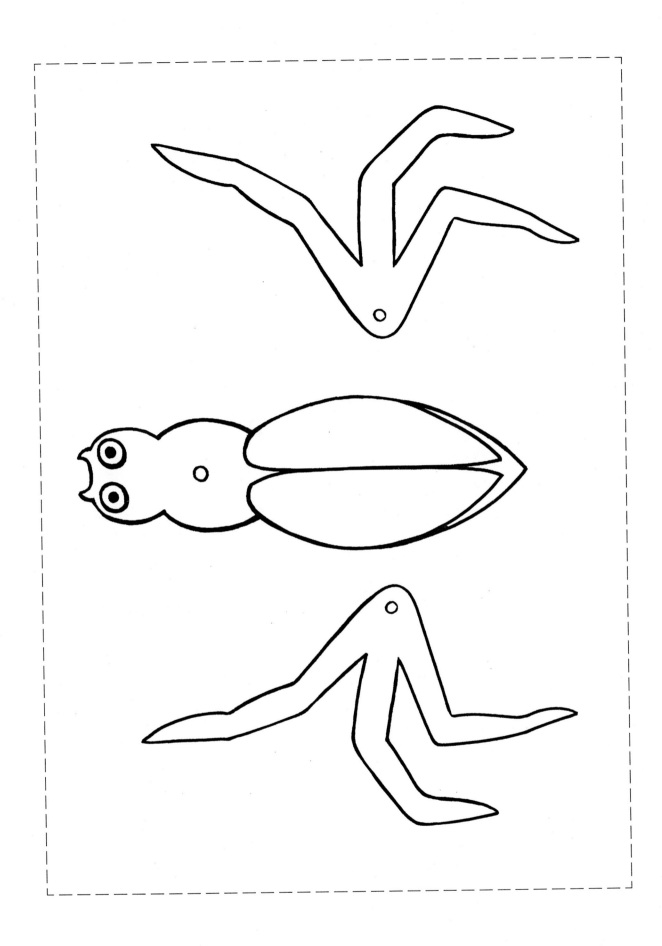

© Essential Resources Educational Publishers Ltd, 2008

Oral Language Plan : Poetry

Title: *Mr Nobody*   **Term:** _____ **Week:** _____

Monday	**Prediction:**
Critical Thinking	What do you do when you have made a mess at home? What is the responsible thing to do?

Tuesday	**Terminology:**
Exploring Language	Verse, rhyming words.
	Vocabulary Development:
	Interest words: mischief, agree, ajar, afar, untidily, scatters. Contractions: there's, it's, don't, they're. Compound words: everybody, afar, ajar, upon, nobody, belong. Singular/plural: door/s, finger/s, plate/s, mouse—mice. Antonyms: quiet—noisy, everybody—nobody, pull—push. Homonyms: know—no, see—sea. Synonyms: mischief—damage, harm, trouble …

Wednesday	**Print Conventions:**
	Capital letters, full stops, commas, exclamation mark.

Thursday	**Phonological Patterns:**
	Word family: ou—mouse, house, round … Blend: pl—plate, play, place … Suffix: ed—cracked, played, scattered … Rhyming words: house—mouse, agree—see, afar—ajar.

Friday	**Visual Information:**
Processing Information	Discuss the italics used for the words "us", "we" and "our" in the last verse.
	Response:
	Use the template on page 12 to copy the door for each child. Colour, cut out and stick the doors into poetry books. Draw the room behind the door. Put a paint handprint onto each door.

Mr Nobody

I know a funny little man,
as quiet as a mouse,
who does the mischief that is done
in everybody's house!
There's no one ever sees his face
and yet we all agree
that every plate we crack was cracked
by Mr Nobody.

It's he who always tears our books,
who leaves the doors ajar;
he pulls the buttons from our shirts
and scatters clothes afar.
That squeaking door will always squeak
for, goodness, don't you see,
we leave the oiling to be done
by Mr Nobody.

The finger marks upon the door
by none of us are made.
We never leave the blinds rolled up
to let the curtains fade.
We never mess and leave our toys
lying untidily.
They're not our toys; they all belong
to Mr Nobody.

© Essential Resources Educational Publishers Ltd, 2008

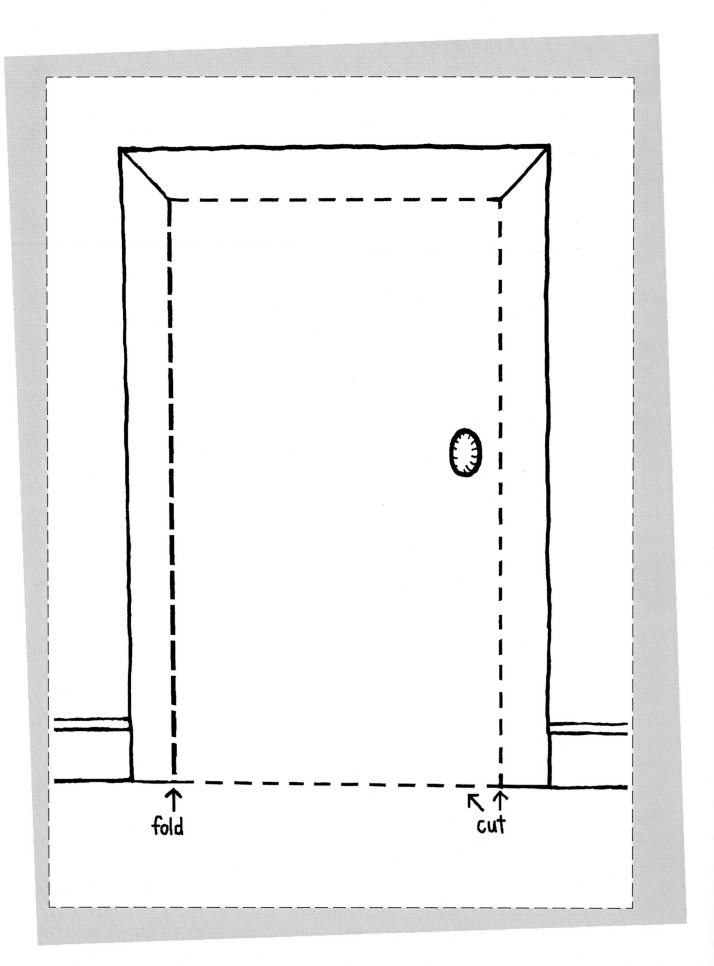

fold

cut

© Essential Resources Educational Publishers Ltd, 2008

Oral Language Plan : Poetry

Title: *The Dog and the Bee*   **Term:** _____ **Week:** _____

Monday Critical Thinking	**Prediction:** What message do you think the poet might be giving us with this poem? How do you think the dog felt at the end of the poem?
Tuesday Exploring Language	**Terminology:** Verse. **Vocabulary Development:** Interest words: settles, winks, sly, tickles, chuckles, spry. Contractions: doesn't, he'll. Compound words: upon, himself. Singular/plural: fly—flies, eye/s, bee/s, toe/s. Antonyms: big—little, tiny—enormous, quick—slow. Homonyms: bee—be, nose—knows, eye—I. Synonyms: big—larger, little—small, chuckles—laughs.
Wednesday	**Print Conventions:** Capital letters, comma, semi-colon, full stop, exclamation mark.
Thursday	**Phonological Patterns:** Word family: og—dog, log, frog … Blend: fl—fly, flies, flew … Suffix: s—winks, chuckles, makes … Rhyming words: toes—nose, fly—sly—eye—spry.
Friday Processing Information	**Visual Information:** Discuss the size of the font used for ouch. **Response:** Use the template on page 15 to copy the dog's face for each child. Colour the dog, cut it out and stick it into the poetry book. Use the template of the bee's body on page 15. Trace and cut out the body on black paper. Collage yellow stripes onto the body. Cut cellophane or bubble wrap wings and staple to the bee's body. Stick the bee onto the dog's nose.

        © Essential Resources Educational Publishers Ltd, 2008

The Dog and the Bee

Great big dog,
Head upon his toes;
Tiny little bee
Settles on his nose.

Great big dog
Thinks it's a fly.
Never says a word,
Winks very sly.

Tiny little bee,
Tickles dog's nose –
Thinks, like as not,
It's a pretty rose.

Dog smiles a smile,
Winks his other eye,
Chuckles to himself
How he'll catch a fly.

Then he makes a snap,
Very quick and spry,
Snaps up the bee.
Ouch! It's not a fly!

© Essential Resources Educational Publishers Ltd, 2008

15

© Essential Resources Educational Publishers Ltd, 2008

Oral Language Plan : Poetry

Title: *Open Sesame*   **Term:** _____ **Week:** _____

Monday	**Prediction:**
Critical Thinking	What do you think this poem might be about? Why ? After reading the poem, assess the predictions.
Tuesday	**Terminology:**
Exploring Language	Verse.
	Vocabulary Development:
	Interest words: open sesame, shady, nook, whispering, overhead, whereon. Compound words: whereon, overhead, indoors. Singular/plural: book/s, leaf—leaves. Antonyms: open—closed, shady—sunny, old—new. Homonyms: new—knew. Synonyms: shady—dim, sheltered, cloudy ...
Wednesday	**Print Conventions:**
	Capital letters, comma, full stop, semi—colon.
Thursday	**Phonological Patterns:**
	Word family: oo—book, nook, look ... Blend: str—street, string, straight ... Suffix: ing—whispering, looking, reading ... Rhyming words: nook—book, out—about, old—gold.
Friday	**Visual Information:**
Processing Information	Discuss the presentation of the words "new" and "old".
	Response:
	Fold A4 size paper as per diagram on page 18. Each child makes their own book—story book, alphabet book, counting book are some suggestions. Ensure each book has a cover with a title and author on it. Stick the finished book onto a page in the poetry book.

Open Sesame

Oh, for a book and a shady nook

Either indoors or out,

With the green leaves whispering overhead,
And
the
wind
blowing
all
about,
Where I may read all at my ease,

Both of the  new and old;

For a jolly good book whereon to look

Is better to me than gold.

© Essential Resources Educational Publishers Ltd, 2008

MAKE A BOOK

① Fold A4 size paper in half.

② Fold in half again...

③ Fold in half again.

④ Now unfold until you are back at step1 with A4 folded in half. Cut from the centre of the fold, to the centre point.

⑤ Open A4 paper and fold in half long ways.

⑥ Push inwards to make a book.

© Essential Resources Educational Publishers Ltd, 2008

Oral Language Plan : Poetry

Title: *The Smile*   **Term:** _____ **Week:** _____

Monday	**Prediction:**
Critical Thinking	What happens when you smile at someone? How does it make you feel when someone smiles at you?

Tuesday	**Terminology:**
Exploring Language	Poet, poem.
	Vocabulary Development:
	Interest words: crinkles, secret, wonderful. Contractions: it's. Singular/plural: face/faces, place/places. Antonyms: smile—frown, lovely—horrible. Homonyms: know—no, to—too—two. Synonyms: wonderful—amazing, awesome, marvellous, astonishing.

Wednesday	**Print Conventions:**
	Capital letter, full stop, dash, exclamation mark.

Thursday	**Phonological Patterns:**
	Word family: ace—face, place, race ... Blend: sm—smile, smart, smell ... Suffix: ing—hide / hiding, ride / riding ... Rhyming words: face—place, do—two.

Friday	**Visual Information:**
Processing Information	Discuss why the poet has shaped the first and last lines.
	Response:
	Use the template on page 21 to make a copy of the face for each child. Colour and cut out the face. Stick it into poetry book. Cut and colour smiling mouth (see template on page 21)and add to the face. Print hair using paint and toothpaste lid—to make curls!

© Essential Resources Educational Publishers Ltd, 2008

A Smile

A smile is such a lovely thing,

It crinkles up your face,
And when it's gone it's hard to find
Its secret hiding place.
But far more wonderful it is
to know what smiles can do –
I smile at you,
You smile at me,

And so, one smile makes two!

© Essential Resources Educational Publishers Ltd, 2008

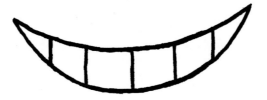

© Essential Resources Educational Publishers Ltd, 2008

Oral Language Plan : Poetry

Title: *The Parrot*　　　　　　　　　　　　　　**Term:** _____ **Week:** _____

Monday	**Prediction:**
Critical Thinking	Prediction: What is a pirate? Where do you think we might find a pirate? What does a parrot look like? What colours are their feathers?
Tuesday	**Terminology:**
Exploring Language	Verse, anonymous.
	Vocabulary Development:
	Interest words: pirate, crow's nest, guard, treasure. Contractions: don't. Compound words: inside. Singular/plural: parrot/s, pirate/s. Antonyms: sleep—wake, brave—scared. Homonyms: sail—sale. Synonyms: guard—protect, save, shelter, watch …
Wednesday	**Print Conventions:**
	Comma, apostrophe, exclamation mark, capital letters.
Thursday	**Phonological Patterns:**
	Phonological Patterns: Word family: ea—sea, meat, treat … Blend: tr—trees, treasure, trip … Suffix: 's—pirate's, crow's, captain's. Rhyming words: seas—trees, bold—gold.
Friday	**Visual Information:**
Processing Information	Discuss the direction of line three in relation to the position of a crow's nest. Discuss the bold font used in line six.
	Response:
	Use the template of the parrot on page 24 to make one parrot for each child. Colour and shade the parrot with pastels. Colour both sides of an A5 piece of paper. Fold the paper concertina style and thread through the parrot at the dotted line to make wings. Draw the top of a treasure chest. Stick the parrot onto the chest.

© Essential Resources Educational Publishers Ltd, 2008

The Parrot

I am the pirate's parrot,

I sail the seven seas,

and sleep inside the crow's nest.

Don't look for me in trees!

I am the pirate's parrot,

a bird both **brave** and **bold**.

I guard the captain's treasure

and count his piles of gold.

© Essential Resources Educational Publishers Ltd, 2008

© Essential Resources Educational Publishers Ltd, 2008

Oral Language Plan : Poetry

Title: *Five Little Mice*　　　　　　　　　　**Term:** _____　**Week:** _____

Monday	**Prediction:**
Critical Thinking	What happens in your house when Mum or Dad sees a mouse? Do we want mice in our houses? Why/why not? What is a good way to get rid of them?

Tuesday	**Terminology:**
Exploring Language	Rhyming couplet, poet, anthology.
	Vocabulary Development:
	Interest words: snug, pantry. Compound words: breadcrumbs, something. Singular/plural: mouse—mice, Antonyms: little—big, high—low, more—less, high—low, quickly—slowly. Homonyms: high—hi, so—sew, see—sea Synonyms: looking—searching, wise—clever.

Wednesday	**Print Conventions:**
	Capital letters, comma, dash, exclamation mark.

Thursday	**Phonological Patterns:**
	Word family: ay—day, play, may ... Blend: br—breadcrumbs Suffix: ing—eating, hiding ... Rhyming words: floor—more, high—pie, at—cat, away—day.

Friday	**Visual Information:**
Processing Information	Discuss the presentation of the word "hide".
	Response:
	Copy the mice picture on page 27 for each child. Colour the picture. Stick five pairs of moveable eyes onto the black space. (Alternatively paint white dots onto the black space if eyes are not available.)

© Essential Resources Educational Publishers Ltd, 2008

FIVE LITTLE MICE

Five little mice on the pantry floor,

looking for breadcrumbs - or something **more**!

Five little mice on the shelf up high

eating so nicely on a pie.

But the big round eyes of the wise old cat

see what the five little mice are at.

Quickly he jumps, but the mice run

and hide in their snug little hole all day!

© Essential Resources Educational Publishers Ltd, 2008

27

© Essential Resources Educational Publishers Ltd, 2008

Oral Language Plan : Poetry

Title: *Peep in the Basket*   **Term:** _____   **Week:** _____

Monday	**Prediction:**
Critical Thinking	How do you look after a cat? What is a baby cat called? Give me a word to describe a kitten.

Tuesday	**Terminology:**
Exploring Language	Verse, poem, anthology, rhyming word.
	Vocabulary Development:
	Interest words: peep, mews, surely, tigery, purr. Contractions: that's, can't. Singular/plural: cat—cats, kitten—kittens, basket—baskets. Antonyms: best—worst. Homonyms: one—won. Synonyms: peep—look, spy, peer ...

Wednesday	**Print Conventions:**
	Capital letter, comma, question mark, exclamation mark, dash.

Thursday	**Phonological Patterns:**
	Word family: eep—peep, keep, sleep ... Blend: st—best, rest, stripe ... Suffix: ly—surely ... Rhyming words: see—me, choose—mews, paws—because, best—rest.

Friday	**Visual Information:**
Processing Information	Discuss the bold font used for "me".
	Response:
	Copy the template on page 30 for each child. Colour and cut out the basket and cats. Cut dotted lines on the basket. Weave four coloured strips of paper through the cut lines on the basket. Stick into poetry book.

© Essential Resources Educational Publishers Ltd, 2008

Peep in the Basket

Peep in the basket,
what do you see?
Five little kittens -
and one is for **me**.

Five little kittens -
which one shall I choose?
The grey one that's purring,
the white one that mews?

The all-over black one,
the black with white paws,
the tigery striped one?
I can't choose because -

Each one, when I pet it,
seems surely the best.
So please keep the basket
and give me the rest!

© Essential Resources Educational Publishers Ltd, 2008

© Essential Resources Educational Publishers Ltd, 2008

Oral Language Plan : Poetry

Title: *The Elephant*   **Term:** _____ **Week:** _____

Monday	Prediction:
Critical Thinking	Give me some words to describe an elephant. Discuss the parts of the elephant's body, particularly the trunk.

Tuesday	Terminology:
Exploring Language	Poet, poem, verse, rhyming words.
	Vocabulary Development:
	Interest words: humongous, mudpack, trumpet, suit. Contractions: it's. Compound words: mudpack, himself. Singular/plural: elephant/s, flower/s, tree/s. Antonyms: up—down. Homonyms: knows—nose. Synonyms: humongous—big, gigantic, enormous ...

Wednesday	Print Conventions:
	Capital letters, commas, full stops, dash, exclamation mark.

Thursday	Phonological Patterns:
	Word family: ee—tree, knee, sneeze ... Blend: tr—tree, trick, trumpet ... Suffix: ness—goodness, happiness ... Rhyming words: nose—toes, trees—sneeze, ground—sound, bath—laugh, fruit—suit.

Friday	Visual Information:
Processing Information	Discuss the size of words "humongous" and "sound", the direction of "down" and the position of "sneeze".
	Response:
	Copy an elephant for each child from the template on page 33. Paint the elephants. Cut the elephants out and stick into poetry books. Paint both sides of a strip of paper—3 x 20 cm—for each elephant. Concertina the strip of paper and stick onto the elephant for a nose/trunk.

© Essential Resources Educational Publishers Ltd, 2008

The Elephant

The elephant has a

humongous nose.

It begins on his head and goes

d
o
w

n   **to his toes.**

He uses it to pick up fruit,
Or give himself a mudpack suit.
It's handy when he has a bath.

He sucks up water—it makes him laugh!

When he trumpets—what a sound!
It makes the fruit fall on the ground!
He sniffs the flowers in the trees,
Oh my goodness—it makes him Sneeze!

© Essential Resources Educational Publishers Ltd, 2008

33

© Essential Resources Educational Publishers Ltd, 2008

Oral Language Plan : Poetry

Title: *The Handsome Hippo*   **Term:** _____ **Week:** _____

Monday	**Prediction:**
Critical Thinking	Where do you think we will find a hippo? What does the word hippopotamus mean? (Greek word for river horse.) Give me some words to describe a hippo.
Tuesday	**Terminology:**
Exploring Language	Anthology, verse.
	Vocabulary Development:
	Interest words: handsomest, hide, wallow, treatment, spectacular, swoon, delight, flight. Contractions: it's, I'm, haven't. Compound words: handsome, around. Singular/plural: tooth—teeth, lady—ladies. Antonyms: beautiful—ugly, cooling—heating. Homonyms: hair—hare. Synonyms: handsome—good looking, beautiful, lovely ...
Wednesday	**Print Conventions:**
	Capital letter, comma, full stop, dash, exclamation mark.
Thursday	**Phonological Patterns:**
	Word family: ow—wallow, swallow, fellow, yellow ... Blend: sp—spoil, spectacular, spin ... Suffix: er / est—small, smaller, smallest ... Rhyming words: round—found, mud—blood, delight—flight.
Friday	**Visual Information:**
Processing Information	Discuss what the shape of the text might represent.
	Response:
	Use the template on page 36 to copy the body of a hippopotamus for each child. Paint and cut out the body. Cut lines on the body (see template) and weave pale pink strips of paper through the body. Stick into poetry book.

© Essential Resources Educational Publishers Ltd, 2008

The Handsome Hippo

I'm a handsome hippo with a beautiful hide
because I play all day long in the mud.
I laugh with delight as I wallow around -
It's the best beauty treatment I've ever found
for smoothing the skin and cooling the blood!

I'm the handsomest hippo, I haven't a hair
to spoil my spectacular skin.
The ladies swim round and swoon with delight
But when I smile, oh! Then they take fright
at the sight of my pearly white teeth and my grin!

© Essential Resources Educational Publishers Ltd, 2008

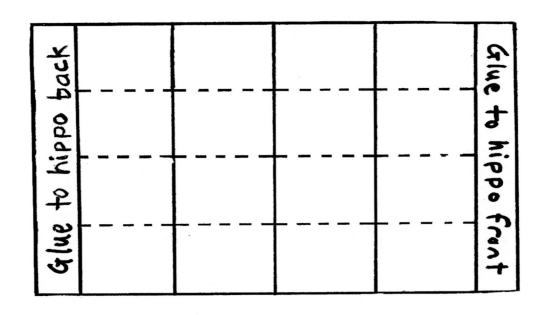

Glue to hippo back

Glue to hippo front

© Essential Resources Educational Publishers Ltd, 2008

36

Oral Language Plan : Poetry

Title: *The Owl*   **Term:** _____ **Week:** _____

Monday Critical Thinking	**Prediction:** What do you know about owls? When do most owls come out to eat?
Tuesday Exploring Language	**Terminology:** Poem, poet, verse, rhyming, anthology. **Vocabulary Development:** Interest words: misty, mournful, motionless, dusky. Compound words: moonlight, motionless. Singular/plural: bird/s, feather/s, creature/s. Antonyms: silent—noisy, misty—clear, night—day. Homonyms: pale—pail, made—maid. Synonyms: motionless—still, statue ...
Wednesday	**Print Conventions:** Capital letters, commas, full stop, dash. Discuss plain punctuation and rich language.
Thursday	**Phonological Patterns:** Word family: own—brown, town, frown ... Blend: gl—glide, glow, glisten ... Suffix: ing—gliding, sleeping ... Rhyming words: night—moonlight, shout—out, eye—sky, brown—town.
Friday Processing Information	**Visual Information:** Discuss the visual presentation of the title. **Response:** Cut out owl and six feather shapes using the templates on page 39. Use pastels to colour the owl and the feather shapes. (Colour feather shapes on both sides.) Fold feather shapes in half and stick onto the body of the owl using PVA glue. Draw stars and a moon on the page in the poetry book. Draw the branch of a tree. Dye the sky a blue/grey colour. Stick the owl onto the branch. Put glitter glue onto the moon.

© Essential Resources Educational Publishers Ltd, 2008

The Owl

It was a silent, misty night.

The wise, old bird

sat motionless in the pale moonlight.

He winked an eye

then flew silently into the

dark, dusky sky.

He spread his feathers,

mottled and brown,

gliding over the sleeping town.

Then he made a mournful shout –

be warned, little creatures,

the owl is out!

© Essential Resources Educational Publishers Ltd, 2008

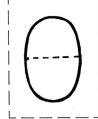

© Essential Resources Educational Publishers Ltd, 2008

Oral Language Plan : Poetry

Title: *Pirate*   **Term:** _____ **Week:** _____

Monday	**Prediction:**
Critical Thinking	What sort of person will we meet in this poem?

Tuesday	**Terminology:**
Exploring Language	Poem, verse, rhyme.
	Vocabulary Development:
	Interest words: treasure, shiver, prickly. Compound words: underground, wherever. Singular/plural: pirate/s, knife—knives, gun/s, man—men. Antonyms: take—give, cry—laugh, big—small. Homonyms: eye—I. Synonyms: treasure—riches, wealth, fortune...

Wednesday	**Print Conventions:**
	Capital letters, full stops, comma, exclamation mark.

Thursday	**Phonological Patterns:**
	Word family: an—man, can, ran ... Blend: tr—treasure, treat, trip ... Suffix: ly—prickly, usually ... Rhyming words: chin—grin, ground—found, gun—run, man—can, eye—cry.

Friday	**Visual Information:**
Processing Information	Discuss the use of different fonts, in particular "evil grin"; the size and boldness of "big black"; and the use of capitals slanting for the word "RUN".
	Response:
	Use the template on page 42 to make a pirate face for each child. Colour and cut out the pirate face. Make an earring out of aluminum foil and thread through the pirate's earlobe. Stick brown wool over his chin for a beard. Stick into poetry book.

© Essential Resources Educational Publishers Ltd, 2008

Pirate

A pirate is a **scary** man,
he **takes his** treasure **from wherever** he can.
He has a patch over **one** eye,
he makes the **children** shiver and **cry**.
He has a **prickly**, *hairy* chin

and usually *smiles* an **evil grin**.

He buries his treasure underground
and *hopes* **IT NEVER** will be **found**.
He carries a knife and a **big black** gun.

When they see him *come*, the people all **RUN!**

© Essential Resources Educational Publishers Ltd, 2008

© Essential Resources Educational Publishers Ltd, 2008

Oral Language Plan : Poetry

Title: *Sounds of the Sea Shore*   **Term:** ___ **Week:** ___

Monday	**Prediction:**
Critical Thinking	What sounds do you think you will hear when you are at the beach? Words to describe the sounds.
Tuesday	**Terminology:**
Exploring Language	Verse, poem, poet, anthology.
	Vocabulary Development:
	Interest words: crunch, swoosh, rat-a-tat, discovered. Compound words: around. Singular/plural: shell/s, bird/s, wave/s, child/ren. Antonyms: white—black, laughing—crying. Homonyms: sea—see, heard—herd, meet—meat. Synonyms: laugh—chuckle, giggle, chortle ...
Wednesday	**Print Conventions:**
	Capital letters, comma, full stop, question mark.
Thursday	**Phonological Patterns:**
	Word family: and—sand, band, hand ... Blend: cr—crunch, crumple, crash ... Suffix: ed—listened, looked ... Rhyming words: shore—more, bird—heard, feet—meet, sand—band, be—me.
Friday	**Visual Information:**
Processing Information	Discuss the representation of the shape of the wavy lines.
	Response:
	Make a bird's eye view of the sea shore in poetry book. Stick blue cellophane on the page as the water. Stick sand onto the rest of the page with PVA glue. Trace white seagull from template on page 45. Cut out and stick feathers on the body. Add to the picture—use a spring, paper fastener or wool if you'd like the bird to move on the page.

© Essential Resources Educational Publishers Ltd, 2008

Sounds of the Sea Shore

Lap, lap go the waves on the sea shore,

Flap, flap go the wings of a white bird.

I listened and then I listened some more,

And these are a few of the sounds I heard.

The crunch of shells under my feet,

The swoosh of water where sea and rocks meet,

The laughter of children digging in sand,

The rat-a-tat from the drummer in the band.

Then I heard singing, oh who can it be?

I looked around and discovered –

It was me!

© Essential Resources Educational Publishers Ltd, 2008

© Essential Resources Educational Publishers Ltd, 2008

Oral Language Plan : Poetry

Title: *Rainbow*   **Term:** ___ **Week:** ___

Monday	**Prediction:**
Critical Thinking	When do we see a rainbow? What colours make up the rainbow? Do they come in a special order? What message is the poet trying to give us?

Tuesday	**Terminology:**
Exploring Language	Poem, rhyming words, anthology, verse.
	Vocabulary Development:
	Interest words: hue, sparkly, arch, reflecting, spy, remind. Compound words: rainbow. Singular/plural: colour/s. Antonyms: new—old, up—down, pale—dark. Homonyms: pale—pail, rain—reign, new—knew. Synonyms: remind—remember, think …

Wednesday	**Print Conventions:**
	Capital letters, comma, full stop, exclamation mark.

Thursday	**Phonological Patterns:**
	Word family: igh—light, might, bright … Blend: sk—sky, skip, skate … Suffix: ed—looked, reminded … Rhyming words: new—blue—hue, sky—spy, light—might.

Friday	**Visual Information:**
Processing Information	Discuss the shape of the words "rainbow arch".
	Response:
	Using oil pastels, draw a rainbow arch—red, orange, yellow, green, blue, indigo and violet. Rub the thumb over the pastel beginning at the red and rubbing towards the violet to shade the colours into one another. Colour the sky with a pale blue dye. White wax clouds could be added before dyeing the sky.

© Essential Resources Educational Publishers Ltd, 2008

Rainbow

The rain had gone, the sky was blue,

the world looked sparkly and oh so new.

As I glanced up towards the sky,

a rainbow arch

I could spy.

The colours ranged from every hue:

the palest yellow to the deepest blue.

A rainbow reflecting all the light

to remind us all of God's great might!

© Essential Resources Educational Publishers Ltd, 2008

Oral Language Plan : Poetry

Title: *The Spider*

Term: ___ Week: __

Monday Critical Thinking	**Prediction:** How many legs does a spider have? How is it different from an insect? Where do you usually find spiders? Where do you think we might find this one?
Tuesday Exploring Language	**Terminology:** Poet, poem, verse. **Vocabulary Development:** Interest words: dreadful, cried. Contractions: can't—cannot. Compound words: sunlight, inside, cannot. Singular/plural: spider/s, leg/s, shoe/s, foot—feet. Antonyms: inside—outside. Homonyms: eight—ate, there—their, need—knead. Synonyms: dreadful—awful, horrible, terrible.
Wednesday	**Print Conventions:** Capital letters, comma, full stop, speech marks, exclamation mark.
Thursday	**Phonological Patterns:** Word family: ide—hide, side, ride ... Blend: sp—spider, speed, sprain ... Suffix: ing—trying, hiding, playing. Rhyming words: sunlight—bright—fright, inside—hide, say—play
Friday Processing Information	**Visual Information:** Discuss the use of the staggered words to show climbing, the font used for "bright sunlight" to show rays of the sun, and the enlarged font to emphasise "fright". **Response:** Use the pattern to make some cardboard templates of the shoe. Trace, colour and cut out the shoe. Cut corrugated cardboard circles. Push four pipe cleaners through the corrugations to make the eight legs of the spider. Attach some string to the spider and to the page. Stick the coloured shoe over the string.

© Essential Resources Educational Publishers Ltd, 2008